ACTIVISM IN ACTION
······ A HISTORY™ ······

THE FIGHT FOR
ANIMAL RIGHTS

JEANNE NAGLE

Rosen
YA™

New York

Published in 2020 by The Rosen Publishing Group, Inc.
29 East 21st Street, New York, NY 10010

Library of Congress Cataloging-in-Publication Data

Names: Nagle, Jeanne, author.
Title: The fight for animal rights / Jeanne Nagle.
Description: First edition. | New York : Rosen Publishing, 2020.
| Series: Activism in action : a history | Includes bibliographi-
cal references and index.
Identifiers: LCCN 2018015267| ISBN 9781508185383 (library
bound) | ISBN 9781508185376 (pbk.)
Subjects: LCSH: Animal rights—Juvenile literature. | Animal
welfare—Juvenile literature.
Classification: LCC HV4708 .N34 2019 | DDC 179/.3—dc23
LC record available at https://lccn.loc.gov/2018015267

Manufactured in China

On the cover: As long as creatures such as rabbits are
subjected to testing, or exploited for their skin and fur, animal
rights activists will speak out on behalf of their nonhuman
counterparts.

CONTENTS

INTRODUCTION

Humans have had a complex relationship with animals for centuries. Some twenty thousand years ago, people's ancient ancestors had only two choices when it came to animals: they either hunted the creatures for food or became the hunted/food themselves. Eventually humans domesticated several species. These tamed animals offered humans protection, companionship, labor, and an easily obtained source of meat and material for clothing. In return, domesticated animals received food and shelter, yet were considered little more than owned property for humans to do with what they pleased.

The lives of animals have intertwined with humans in many ways that have been beneficial to the latter, although not the former. Abuse of pets and farm animals is one such case in point. In the name of "sport," animals have been hunted or pitted against each other in fights to the death. They have been taken out of the wild and put on display in zoos and circuses. Experiments have been conducted on live animals by those seeking better ways to treat humans.

Humans have long hunted animals for food, and sometimes for "fun." Animal rights activists have been known to object to all forms of hunting.

In the 1800s, people began to advocate on behalf of mistreated animals. In the United States, animal welfare organizations, such as the American Society for the Prevention of Cruelty to Animals and the Humane Society, focused on protecting animals by reducing or alleviating their suffering. In the 1970s, some animal advocates took things a step further by also campaigning to win for animals some of the same rights that humans enjoyed. Chief among these were the freedom from suffering and the right to be worthy of consideration as living beings, not just things to be owned. Thus the animal rights movement was born.

Animal welfare is defined by humans as having compassion for what they consider lesser living things. On one hand, animal welfarists try to ensure that animals are treated well as they serve or otherwise benefit humans. The animal rights movement, on the other hand, also believes that animals are living beings that are "other than" instead of "lesser than" humans. Animal rights advocates believe animals deserve to live free from the threat of harm at the hands of humans, no matter what form that harm might take. Members of the animal rights movement argue that just as humans cannot legally use or take advantage of other people, they should not have the right to harm or use animals for their own benefit.

Some factions of the animal rights movement have used destructive and illegal means to make their case. Many others, however, have stuck with methods that have proven effective for other social justice causes, such as the civil rights movement and a host of human rights efforts. Working to pass favorable laws, enforc-ing existing legislation, publishing scientific findings that support their beliefs, protesting, and speaking out are some of the more common ways animal rights advocates have gained sup-port for their cause. Anyone who chooses to join the animal rights movement should be ready, willing, and able to participate in these, and other peaceful yet effective means, in order to make a difference.

CHAPTER ONE

HUMAN AND NONHUMAN ANIMALS

. . . . ● ● ● ● ● ● ● . . . .

B iologically speaking, people and animals are actually a part of one big family. Within the scientific classification of living things, which groups organisms according to their similarities and differences, humans are listed in the same "kingdom" as animals. That means that at the highest cellular level, human and nonhuman animals have a lot in common. It is only by going deeper into the classification system, called taxonomy, that one can see how science separates animals one from the other. Discussions concerning animal rights often hinge on such similarities and differences that run through the animal kingdom.

Science is not the only avenue for the animal rights debate. Philosophers have weighed in on the matter for ages. Their concerns revolve not so much around biological makeup as around ethics and morality. Deciding what is morally right or wrong when it comes to the treatment of animals is also the approach taken by various religions and spiritual groups.

HIGH AND MIGHTY

Within the taxonomic system, humans are among a group of animals known as primates, which comes from the Latin word for "chief" or "first rank." Primates receive such a high rank because they possess many helpful adaptations, including brains that are large for their body size. Human brains also have a vast number of neurons, which allow the brain to function at a very high level. Additionally, the complex way in which all these neurons act in the human brain increases cognitive ability, meaning being able to understand and learn.

With all these great things going for them, naturally humans would think that they were superior to other animals—even other primates, such as gorillas and chimpanzees. Animal rights advocates claim that this feeling of humans being "greater than" has led to what they call "speciesism." Coined by philosopher Richard Ryder and studied by animal rights icon Peter Singer, speciesism is an important term in the language of animal rights. By virtue of believing themselves to be the most important, or even the only important, species, humans have given themselves an excuse to basically do whatever they want to all the animals that are below them. Using nonhuman

SHARE AND SHARE ALIKE

Humans might put themselves above the animals, but genetically speaking, they are not so different from their fellow members of the animal kingdom. As fellow primates, humans and the great apes are closely related through DNA. Testing has shown that people share more than 98 percent of their DNA with chimpanzees, gorillas, and a type of chimp called bonobos. Orangutans and monkeys share less DNA with humans, but the percentage is still significant—96 and 93 percent, respectively.

Various studies have hinted that other animals

Science has determined that, in evolutionary and/or genetic terms, certain species of nonhuman animals are quite similar to humans. Chimpanzees are high on that list.

beyond primates also are genetically similar to humans. In order of the highest to lowest amount of shared DNA, other mammals include cats, mice, dogs, and cows. As for birds, people are most closely related to chickens. Their 60 percent DNA similarity with humans is equal to that of a surprising member of the plant family—bananas.

animals for their own benefit and treating them poorly is justified in their minds. Animal rights advocates maintain that speciesism is the same as racism and sexism—and it is just as wrong. The argument is that the differences between animals and humans qualify the former to be considered "other than," not "lesser than."

FEELING AND DOING GOOD

As a species that is high up in the hierarchy of living things, humans naturally assume superiority in many areas. They believe that they alone possess certain characteristics that set them apart from their nonhuman animal kin. Two traits that are important when considering animal rights are sentience and moral standing. Sentience is the ability to feel emotions and pain, and to be aware of oneself and one's surroundings. A somewhat simplified definition of moral standing is how worthy a person or thing is of being treated in an ethical manner.

In his book *An Introduction to the Principles of Morals and Legislation* (1789), English philosopher Jeremy Bentham discusses how humans and animals are treated differently under the law. He wrote: "The day may come, when the rest of the animal creation may acquire those rights which never could have been withholden from them but by the hand of tyranny. ... The question is not can they *reason*? nor, can they *talk*? but, can they *suffer*?" His line of reasoning was that if animals are sentient, meaning able to feel pain, then they can and do suffer, often at the hands of the human "tyrants" who oppress them.

Modern scientific evidence has indicated that animals are, indeed, sentient. Researchers have observed the behavior of animals experiencing hunger, pain, or distress; examined magnetic resonance imaging (MRI) scans done on the brains of animals (dogs, specifically) while they were seeing a familiar person or hearing that person's voice; and gauged spikes in heartbeat and brainwaves in cows that had successfully completed a test to find food. Findings from these and other studies, as well as evidence from studies into the evolution of various species, have convinced scientists and the general public that animals feel positive and negative emotions.

Animal rights advocates argue that, as sentient beings, nonhuman animals are deserving of

Portrait of Jeremy Bentham, one of the first philosophers to raise questions that would support the rise of the animal rights movement.

moral standing. After all, if animals think, feel, comprehend, and express emotions, it is safe to say that they have a vested interest in their own well-being. Ethical considerations demand that good, or moral, people take into account the needs and desires of others. Animal rights advocates take that statement a step further by saying it makes no difference if those "others" are people or animals. Therefore, the animal rights movement involves more than simply taking an interest in animals. Members of the movement are dedicated to analyzing and supporting the interests of the animals themselves.

OTHER MARKERS

There are a number of other factors that come into play when determining whether or not animals are entitled to rights. In many cases, scientists and philosophers have determined what they believe are special qualities humans have that afford them certain rights, and then applied those conditions to nonhuman animals. Among these are the abilities to reason and learn, communicate through language, and be self-aware. Animal rights advocates point out that evidence of these traits in animals can be found through scientific testing and ordinary everyday observation.

UNEXPECTED TEST RESULTS

In a strange twist of fate, it turns out that non-harmful, carefully monitored experiments may play a crucial role in stopping animal experiments that are deemed cruel and inhumane. Thousands of studies on different nonhuman species over the past three decades have proven that animals

Canine protesters outside United Nations headquarters in New York City help drive home the message that animal testing is considered by many to be a cruel and inhumane practice.

(continued on the next page)

(continued from the previous page)

are capable of feeling and experiencing emotion. Backed by science, animal rights advocates can effectively argue that as sentient beings like humans, animals are entitled to live free from fear and pain. By doing so, this puts an end to live animal experimentation.

REASONING AND LEARNING

Animal test subjects who have shown a preference to living space that has "extras," such as toys or bedding, over bare-bones accommodations are said to be using preferential reasoning. They are choosing to be more entertained or comfortable. Rats have been conditioned to avoid going to one end of "T" maze after being shocked when moving in that direction, which scientists say shows they can learn and remember. Birds use deception, such as pretending to have a broken wing or imitating another prey animal, in order to distract predators and keep their nests safe. On the observational end, many pet owners have watched as their dogs and cats have found clever ways to sneak a treat, even when the food is placed out of reach or merely hidden in a cabinet.

LANGUAGE SKILLS

Likewise, different species of nonhuman animals communicate using sounds and vocal signals that many scientists recognize as language. Just because it does not sound like human speech and people do not understand, animal rights advocates say, does not mean animal language is not legitimate. They also point out that there are cases of animals speaking using human vocabulary. Koko, a gorilla who could sign more than two thousand words, and a parrot named Alex, who spoke

Alex the grey parrot could identify colors and shapes as well as verbally communicate with researcher Dr. Irene Pepperberg and other humans. Alex died in 2007.

more than one hundred words and was able to carry on conversations, are well-known animals with impressive language skills.

SELF-AWARENESS

In a study conducted in 2001, researchers discovered that dolphins were able to recognize themselves in mirrors. Furthermore, they were greatly interested in checking out marks researchers had applied to their bodies, repeatedly examining their new "makeup" in the mirror. A 2015 study, using a larger number of dolphins, concluded that these mammals not only recognized their own mirror images, but did so at an earlier age than most human children. In both cases, researchers hailed their findings as proof that dolphins were self-aware. Similar studies, with much the same results, have been conducted on elephants, parrots, and primates.

ANCIENT AND EARLY ANIMAL "WISDOM"

In their search for great and deep wisdom about the nature of life, philosophers frequently tackle questions having to do with ethics. The matter of animal rights and welfare is one such subject that has been considered and debated for centuries. The Ancient Greek philosopher and mathematician Pythagoras (500–490 BCE) was among the first whose beliefs on this matter have been recorded. Pythagoras and his followers believed that animals deserved respect and compassion from humans based mainly on the belief that animals, like humans, had souls. Not only that, but the souls of humans and animals were interchangeable after death, in a form of reincarnation. In other words, in one life, a soul could exist inside an animal, only to come back in the next life in human form, and vice versa. Therefore, smart humans were kind to animals so that they would not risk receiving negative payback in another life.

Plato (427–327 BCE) and his student Aristotle (384–322 BCE) also believed that animals had souls, but they were not interchangeable with, nor equal to, human souls. Therefore, humans were the superior, "immortal" beings, and animals lived to be of service to them. Aristotle also held that only humans had the ability to reason, and so were superior to nonhuman creatures. Animals had a certain level of awareness about their own lives, but as inferior beings, they must give in to the will of humans. The Stoics, ancient Greek and Roman philosophers who believed living the best life included self-control, reason, and nature,

Statue of Greek philosopher Aristotle. Several of the ancients believed humans were superior to animals based on the ability to reason and possesion of a favored soul.

agreed. They thought animals were put on Earth to serve humankind.

Plenty of early philosophical input revolved around the moral implications, to humans, of treating animals well or poorly. Depending on what school of philosophy was being followed, philosophers generally saw animals as either unfeeling creatures not worthy of people's undue care or concern, possessions whose only role in life was to serve humankind, or lowly creatures people should care for to protect their own moral and earthly interests. Notable for his philosophical take on animals was René Descartes (1596–1650), who believed animals were not worthy of consideration because they were like machines—incapable of independent thought, emotions, or even the physical sensation of pain. German philosopher Immanuel Kant (1724–1894) seemed to suggest that humans should be kind to animals so that they did not slide down a slippery moral slope toward treating humans poorly as well.

INTO THE ANIMAL RIGHTS AGE

By the 1970s, philosophers had begun to see the topic of animal welfare in a new light. Philosophical discussions moved from focusing on care and treatment exclusively, to the matter of whether or not animals, like humans, had rights. Peter Singer (1946–) was among the first modern philosophers to examine and address the issue of animals' moral status. His stance, detailed in his 1975 book, *Animal Liberation*, has been that by virtue of their sentience, animals had the right to be treated in a way that either minimizes their pain and suffering or gets rid of it altogether. His animal rights philosophy stems from the utilitarian belief that people should work to act in such ways that bring more joy into the world and lessen suffering. While Singer was decidedly against speciesism and "factory farming," he did not believe that animals should have the same rights as humans, merely the same consideration as people would give one another.

With regard to animal rights, Tom Regan (1938–) comes from another philosophical camp. Regan declares that animals are not only sentient, but they also are capable of learning and reasoning. He coined the term "subject of a life" to describe the value animals possessed in their own right, beyond being useful to humans, and therefore subject to moral standing and certain rights.

CHAPTER TWO

BATTLEGROUNDS AND BATTLES

A nimal advocates have never been shy when it comes to speaking out against what they consider to be cases of injustice. Beatings, abandonment, experimentation, overwork, horrible living conditions, and inhumane methods of slaughter are among the offenses that have made animal lovers angry and concerned enough to act. In England and the United States, the organized animal welfare movement began in the nineteenth century when compassionate people sought to make life better for wagon-pulling horses. Efforts quickly spread to encompass live animals being cut open and otherwise experimented upon, as well as animals being raised for food.

Consequently, the fight for animal rights has been fought on several fronts, and it is still being fought today. The battlegrounds on which this war is being waged include laboratories, circuses, theme parks, farms, and family homes

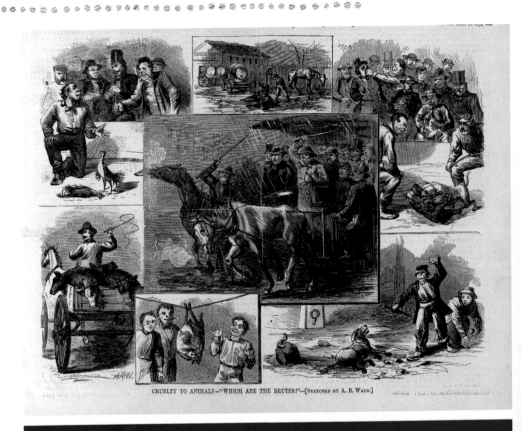

CRUELTY TO ANIMALS—"WHICH ARE THE BRUTES?"—[SKETCHED BY A. R. WAUD.]

An illustration from *Harper's Weekly* magazine depicting several forms of animal cruelty. Shown are illegal fighting, overwork, physical violence, and cruel slaughter methods.

with dinner tables. Along the way, the animal rights movement has scored a number of victories toward stopping mistreatment and gaining support for the movement.

CRUEL AND NOT SO UNUSUAL

Cruelty, which encompasses physical harm, abandonment, and neglect, forms the unfortunate cornerstone of the animal welfare movement. Welfare groups, such as the American Society for the Prevention of Cruelty to Animals (ASPCA) and the Humane Society of the United States (HSUS), focus on the right of animals to live free from fear and suffering. They make it their mission to rescue animals in need, get them medical treatment (if necessary), and find them new and loving homes. Acting on tips from concerned citizens, these groups protect house pets, strays, animals in illegal fighting and breeding operations, and live-stock (animals kept or raised for people to use in some way).

In order for welfare groups to operate efficiently, legally, and successfully, they frequently work to pass and uphold legislation that helps protect animals and punish their abusers. Cruelty cases also stem from, or have some kind of crossover with, other animal welfare and rights battlegrounds, especially cases involving animal experimentation and animals used for entertainment or sport.

EXPERIMENTATION

People have been experimenting on animals since around 300 BCE, the time of the ancients. The practice of vivisection, where surgery was performed on live animals—often without anes-thetic—was fairly common in the 1800s. Doctors and scientists operated on animals to determine how muscles and organs worked. In the twentieth and twenty-first centuries, animals acted as stand-ins for humans during experiments that could have resulted in grave injury or death.

Animal rights advocates have a long history of battling the use of mammals in lab experiments. In fact, objections to animal experimentation have played an important role in the animal rights movement. For instance, the Humane Society of the United States was created after cofounder Fred Myers broke with leadership from the American Humane Society over the practice of surrendering homeless animals for use in medical studies. Plenty of pro-animal legislation has included penalties for inhumane experimentation. Also, pressure from animal advocates has convinced several companies to discontinue the use of animals in their product testing.

THAT'S ENTERTAINMENT?

Circuses, zoos, aquariums, and marine parks attract thousands of eager spectators in the United States each year. Chances are, however, there are not many animal rights advocates among the folks who make up the delighted audiences. In fact, members of the animal rights movement are

While fascinating to watch up close, creatures kept in aquariums and zoos are not in their natural habitats, and therefore may be thought of as abused.

far more likely to protest outside such places than they are to go inside and enjoy the show. From an animal rights standpoint, the animals that perform and inhabit such entertainment locations are not living free, natural lives. Zoos, they say, are actually animal prisons, and even the largest aquarium tanks cannot come close to the wide-open bodies of water that house sea creatures in the wild. Furthermore, there have been claims that sometimes

RIDE 'EM (HUMANELY), COWBOY!

Rodeos also have come under fire from animal rights groups for being an inhumane form of entertainment. Chief among the advocates' concerns are the methods used to get a dramatic reaction from steers, bulls, and horses. Electric prods and sharp, tight straps cause the animals stress and pain, which makes them more aggressive than they normally would be. The more they buck and thrash about, the better the show for the audience. Animals are also at risk of injury during rodeo events, such as roping and riding. Organizers point out that there are many rules and regulations governing rodeos. Yet some states and cities in which rodeos are held place additional rules on these events in an effort to protect the animals.

animals, such as circus elephants and marine park whales, are mistreated in the course of learning how to perform tricks.

The argument has been made that zoos, aquariums, and the like serve an educational purpose, where the public can observe and learn about various species that they might otherwise encounter only in books. Such places also are credited with promoting wildlife conservation efforts. Animal rights advocates respond by claiming that the harm done to animals in entertainment outweighs any such benefits.

A SPORTING CHANCE

Some factions of the animal rights movement also discourage people from supporting sporting events that feature animals as the main attraction. Such events include horse races, greyhound races, and animal fighting operations. Animal racing is big business. Horse and greyhound owners make money based on how well their "athletes" perform. Consequently, the temptation to produce winners

Allegations of abuse and mistreatment are frequently raised against greyhound tracks. Training methods and what happens to dogs once they "retire" are hot-button topics.

is great, oftentimes resulting in excess training and abuse disguised as motivational techniques. The use of performance-enhancing drugs, which are illegal and possibly harmful, can also be part of the equation. Injuries are common in animal racing. Horses and dogs that get injured, or do not win enough races, are often put down or destroyed. Groups such as People for the Ethical Treatment of Animals (PETA) and Grey2K USA Worldwide have urged that these "sports" be outlawed for the safety of the animals.

Animal rights groups have also done what they can to put an end to the underground blood sports of dog fighting and cockfighting. These events pit specially trained animals against each other in a fight that is quite literally to the death. Despite the fact that running an animal fighting operation is illegal in every US state (a felony in most), these kinds of activities still exist because there is big money to be made. Owners of winning dogs and roosters get a cut of the profits from bets made by spectators.

MURDER-FREE CONSUMPTION

Animal rights advocates object to animals being farmed for food on a couple of different levels, not the least of which is the problem of humans killing fellow sentient beings and eating their flesh. Many animal rights advocates are vegetarians or vegans, meaning they do not eat animal flesh, or they forego eating or using any animal products at all, respectively. Animal products include food (meat, eggs, dairy, and honey) and nonfood (fur, wool, and leather) items. In addition to their own restricted consumption of animal products, some vegetarians and vegans choose to join the animal rights movement by promoting their animal- or animal product-free lifestyle within the general public.

Animal rights advocates are generally adamant in their belief that animals should not be "murdered" to accommodate the wishes and desires of humans. However, in the absence of being able to stop the farming of animals for food, animal welfare advocates have made a point of pushing for humane methods of slaughter.

Also near the top of that list of animal rights concerns are the conditions in which farm animals are kept. In order to stay competitive, much of the farming industry has turned to industrial animal production, or "factory farming," where the rights of animals are ignored in favor of turning a profit. This involves housing a large number of animals in very small pens, stalls, or cages. Livestock-centered arms of the animal rights movement have placed adequate housing and humane treatment for farm animals high on their agendas.

WORKING FOR THE MAN

There was a time when animals played a crucial part in getting work done. Farmers counted on horses, oxen, and similar creatures to pull equipment that allowed them to plant and harvest in the field. They also needed these animals to pull the carts and wagons that brought their goods to market, and transported themselves from place to place. History has shown that these animals were not always treated with the utmost care and respect. In return for their hard work, they might be whipped or driven to exhaustion.

What started out as a handful of animal welfare advocates intervening when they witnessed such mistreatment, gave working horses, in particular, a fighting chance at a better life. They petitioned state and local governments for the right to investigate claims of abuse, bringing charges against offenders, erecting watering stations in some cities, and even starting an ambulance service to take injured horses in for medical care.

Gone are the days when people used horses as their main form of transportation in the United States and most European nations. Today humans travel by car and transport goods over roads using motorized trucks. Tractors and other farm machinery have replaced a strong steed pulling

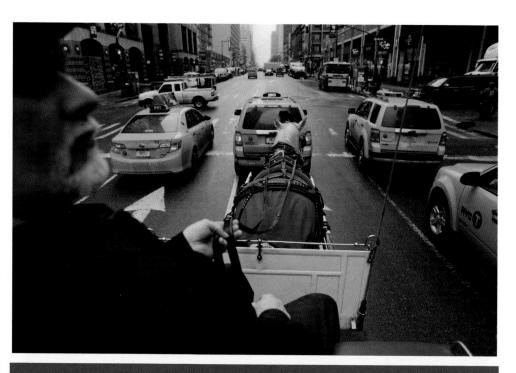

A hansom cab ride through the streets of New York City, from the viewpoint of the driver. The fate of such working horses is debated in several places.

a plow. But there are still examples of horses that are used as working animals. For instance, rides in horse-drawn carriages, called hansom cabs, are a big attraction in some cities. The carriages typically operate, at least in part, on busy city streets with cars whizzing by. Claiming unsafe working conditions, animal rights advocates have called for a ban on hansom cabs, sometimes offering alternatives, such as open-air motor carriages. Advocacy groups, on behalf of carriage drivers and the cities in which they operate, have pushed back. They have launched their own campaigns, emphasizing the humane way in which the horses are handled and cared for, as well as regulations in place to ensure their safety.

ADOPTION OF THE FIVE FREEDOMS

In 1964, Ruth Harrison shined a light on factory farming practices in England with the publication of her book, *Animal Machines*. People were shocked to learn that, instead of roaming around pastures and barnyards freely, animals were confined to small cages or spaces, valued only for how much and how quickly they could produce. The book caused such outrage that the following year the British government issued a report outlining required changes that would make farming more humane. England's Farm Animal Welfare Council adopted and expanded upon recommendations made in the report to create what is known as the Five Freedoms:

1. Freedom from hunger and thirst by ready access to fresh water and a diet to maintain full health and vigor.
2. Freedom from discomfort by providing an

appropriate environment, including shelter and a comfortable resting area.

3. Freedom from pain, injury, or disease by prevention or rapid diagnosis and treatment.
4. Freedom to express normal behavior by providing sufficient space, proper facilities, and company of the animal's own kind.
5. Freedom from fear and distress by ensuring conditions and treatment, which avoid mental suffering.

ACTING ON ANIMAL WELFARE

The Animal Welfare Act of 1966 was created to oversee the commercial use of animals in the United States, driven largely by a need to regulate the way animal testing laboratories were run. Under the act, which was the first federal act of its kind in the United States, labs that conducted testing on live animals were required to be registered with the government, and the dealers who sold animals to them had to be licensed. This latter requirement was designed to stop, or at least reduce, the number of pets that were stolen and sold to testing facilities, which was an increasingly significant problem at the time. Initial wording of the act covered the sale and use of commonly stolen pets such as cats and dogs, but also guinea pigs, hamsters, and rabbits. Monkeys were not pets, but they were commonly used as test subjects, so the law provided for them, as well.

As the times have changed, so has the Animal Welfare Act. As of 2018, the law has been amended eight times. The first amendment, in 1970, broadened the scope of animals protected under the law, including additional "warm-blooded" creatures, such as mice, rats, and birds. (A 2002 amendment to the law excluded those three animals from protection.) It also subjected animal exhibitors, including circuses and zoos, and breeders to many of the same regulations it originally had placed upon animal dealers. Additionally, testing labs were required to conduct experiments humanely, which included giving animals painkillers—provided that doing so did not interfere with the experiment at hand.

Later amendments plugged holes in the language of the act as they became apparent. These included the transportation and handling of lab animals; the formation of testing oversight committees with at least one objective member chosen from the general public; a mandatory five-day waiting period before a group or organization could sell stray and "unwanted" animals to a lab, so that stolen pets could possibly be recovered; living conditions of test animals; and

BARNYARD PROTECTIONS

For a long time, farm animals in America seemed to have gotten a raw deal. As it is written, the Animals Welfare Act excludes livestock, and no other federal law addresses them specifically. Laws protecting farm animals are generally left to the states, and animal rights advocates claim such measures have spotty records of success in this area. The Animal Legal Defense Fund notes that farm animals often are excluded from state anti-cruelty laws. The closest livestock has come to achieving federal protection is being covered under laws that govern how animals are transported and slaughtered. Even so, birds have largely been excluded from these protections.

In addition to attempts to get laws passed protecting livestock, the animal rights movement is active in combating what are known as "ag-gag" laws. These are laws that make it illegal to conduct undercover investigations into cruel farming and inhumane slaughter practices. As of 2018, six states had active ag-gag laws in place. According to the Humane Society of the United States, nearly five times as many of these laws have been defeated in other states.

a call for additional oversight of animal dealers who were not a part of official breeding facilities.

ANIMAL RIGHTS AROUND THE WORLD

When the European Union (EU) was first formed in the 1990s, the European Parliament approved a "treaty declaration," provided by the group Compassion in World Farming, stating that animals were sentient beings. The declaration served mainly as a guideline, and was not legally binding on member nations. In 2009, the EU approved the Lisbon Treaty, which amended and essentially updated previous international agreements that had been the basis of forming the Union. One change that was made under the Lisbon Treaty delighted animal rights advocates around the world. Animal sentience was upgraded from a declaration to an Article, making it more likely that member nations would alter their farming practices accordingly.

In 2012, neuroscientists at the Francis Crick Memorial Conference at Cambridge University issued the Cambridge Declaration on Consciousness, which stated that the overwhelming majority of nonhuman animals were sentient. That means the scientists were formally acknowledging that animals were consciously aware of, and capable of reacting to, what was happening to them and around them—much like their human counterparts.

Canada last passed federal animal welfare legislation in 1892. Some protections are granted to animals under the country's Criminal Code, but those sections cover animals as property. Animal rights advocates have been trying for nearly two decades, with very little success, to get a law in

PETA members protesting outside Toronto's Eaton Centre. The animal rights movement maintains a strong presence in Canada.

the books that considers animals in their own right as sentient living beings. Canadian animal rights groups have logged more wins with the passage of laws in several of the country's provinces. But even these measures have not been comprehensive enough to suit those in the animal rights movement, and so the fight continues.

THE RISE OF HABEAS CORPUS

Lawyers have successfully argued that certain corporations should be considered "legal persons." Such a ruling obviously does not make these companies human, but it does require courts to treat them as if they were, instead of mere things that do not have rights. Attorney and animal rights advocate Steven Wise figures if corporations can be persons, why not living, sentient animals? In 2013, Wise and the legal team at the Nonhuman Rights Project broke new ground in the fight for animal rights by filing a writ of habeas corpus on behalf of a client he said should be considered a legal person—a chimpanzee named Tommy. Habeas corpus concerns the right of legal persons to be granted their freedom from unlawful imprisonment. Wise argued that Tommy was unlawfully locked in a cage inside a concrete shed in upstate New York. He wanted the chimp released so that he could live out his life in a Florida sanctuary.

Tommy's case seems to have opened the door to this type of legal approach. The Nonhuman Rights Project has filed writs on behalf of three other chimps, one (Kiko) in a situation similar to Tommy's, and the other two (Hercules and Leo) that were being held in a State University of New York at Stony Brook research laboratory. In 2017, the group also filed on behalf of three elephants

President of the Nonhuman Rights Project Steven Wise participates in a 2015 hearing on whether to grant habeas corpus to two chimpanzees, Hercules and Leo.

(Beulah, Karen, and Minnie) being kept, and reportedly abused, by workers at a family-owned zoo in Connecticut. The cases for Tommy, Kiko, and the elephants were denied, and as of 2018 all were under appeal. The judge at a hearing set in the case of Hercules and Leo ruled against them. Soon after, the two chimps were moved to a research facility in Louisiana, thus taking them out of New York state jurisdiction and effectively putting an end to the case.

However, habeas corpus has been successfully argued on behalf of an orangutan named Sandra and a chimpanzee named Cecelia, in Argentina, as well as Chucho the Colombian bear. There was some confusion as to whether or not Sandra had actually been awarded her writ; regardless, she remains in captivity. Chucho's writ was later denied by Colombia's Supreme Court. Cecelia, however, was eventually freed and sent to live in a Brazilian sanctuary.

CHAPTER THREE

NOTEWORTHY FIGURES

M any current actors, writers, musicians, and other celebrities have spoken out in favor of animal rights. Their involvement brings attention to the movement, and may lead their fans to join the cause, as well. Yet it is the contributions of philosophers, scientists, aristocrats, and ordinary caring citizens that have had the most impact on how the movement has evolved.

EVOLUTION AND OTHER CONNECTIONS

Although he was by no means an animal rights activist, Charles Darwin (1809–1882) conducted scientific research that showed connections between human and nonhuman animals. His work helped pave the way for many of the arguments made by modern animal rights advocates. Darwin is most famous for his groundbreaking *Origin of the Species*, in which he maintained that various species of animals descended from common ancestors, adapting in various ways to suit their environments. But it was in his 1871 work, *The Descent of Man*, which fueled what would become the animal rights fire. In this book, Darwin pointed out that "higher animals," or highly developed creatures such as great apes, have physical similarities to humans—no doubt because of their common ancestry.

Furthermore, he wrote that his research had led him to conclude that animals also shared mental, social, and emotional traits with humans. Included in this list were dreaming, which Darwin believed showed animals had imagination, and the play of young animals, indicating the ability to feel happy. Also among the similarities he noted were reactions to fear and motherly love. In general, animals felt pleasure and pain, and as such, were sentient. Nonhuman animals were not much different from their human counterparts, which later animal advocates would claim entitled them to certain human rights.

"THE TRIMATES"

Three dedicated ethnologists—who also happen to be women—are responsible for helping to pave the way for animal rights advocates with regard to some of humans' closest animal relatives:

Jane Goodall overseeing mealtime for three chimps at a reserve in Nairobi in the 1990s. Goodall's role has moved from primate researcher to animal rights and welfare advocate.

primates. Jane Goodall (1934–), Dian Fossey (1933–1985), and Birute Galdikas (1946–) have conducted long-term, fruitful research in the lives of chimpanzees, gorillas, and orangutans, respectively.

Over the course of fifty years, Goodall documented that chimpanzees have a unique, layered social system and a language all their own. She also learned that chimps fashion tools to help them gather food and eat—a fact that animal

BIRDS OF A FEATHER

A fashion craze was killing off thousands of birds each year in the late 1800s. Ladies of the Victorian era took to wearing hats decorated with bird feathers; some hats featured other parts of the birds as well. Some species of bird, such as egrets, were nearly hunted to extinction in a bid to meet demand for the decorated hats. Socialite Harriet Hemenway formed the Massachusetts Audubon Society, which launched a boycott of feathered hats. The organization got the state's legislature to outlaw the use of wild bird feathers in clothing, hats, and other merchandise. Following Hemenway's lead, women in other states started similar societies whose members sought to protect birds and their feathers. Pressure from these groups led to the passage of laws protecting wild bird habitats from poachers and hunters. Hemenway is also credited with starting a trend toward nonprofit groups purchasing tracts of land to establish wildlife sanctuaries. In 1922, the Massachusetts Audubon Society created the Moose Hill Wildlife Sanctuary, which is still in operation today.

Animals have long suffered in the name of fashion. This early twentieth-century advertisement for a store in London shows bird feathers adorning hats worn by women in fur coats.

rights advocates have said shows they are more like humans than was previously thought. Critics have faulted Goodall for giving her research subjects names and committing other acts that critics have said are attempts to make chimpanzees seem more like humans than they actually are. While she does not approve of the negative methods used by extreme animal rights groups, she has shown support for activists who fight for the humane treatment of all living creatures.

Fossey consulted with Goodall before setting up camp in Africa to begin her research. She spent the majority of nearly twenty years in the Democratic Republic of Congo and Rwanda studying gorillas by actively living among them. Upon close examination of how the gorillas interacted, Fossey discovered that these primates formed families, bonded with and defended members of those families, mourned losses, and communicated with each other through patterns of vocal calls and chest thumping. Like Goodall with the chimpanzees, Fossey named the gorillas she studied, growing very close to them. She was known to take strong measures against threats to the gorillas, including destroying traps and threatening poachers and their families.

Like Goodall and Fossey, Galdikas was hand-picked by famed anthropologist Louis Leakey to conduct her research. The least known of the so-called Trimates, Galdikas has spent forty years in Indonesia studying orangutans in the forests of Borneo. Her findings on their social structure and mating habits have not so much "humanized" orangutans, as Goodall and Fossey did for their study subjects. Instead, her work has introduced the beasts to a wider audience, inspiring animal welfare and animal rights advocates in the fight to protect the species and their native habitat.

SECRET ANIMAL AGENT

In 1964, the Humane Society of the United States (HSUS) hired a former Army Medical Corps surgical nurse to investigate the illegal lab animal trade in Washington, DC. That man, R. Dale Hylton (1930–2008), would go on to head the organization's humane-education and outreach division. He also was instrumental in the passage of the Animal Welfare Act of 1966. Posing as an animal dealer, Hylton went undercover to expose secret auctions where people were selling cats and dogs to medical labs for experimentation. The secrecy of the auctions was designed to keep owners whose pets had been stolen by dealers from finding their lost animal companions. Hylton's reports on the auctions changed laws in Pennsylvania, where the sales took place, regarding the need for a license to sell of animals. Later his testimony on the matter in front of Congress resulted in the passage of the Animal Welfare Act, which was the first federal law concerning the treatment of animals.

When a dog dealer successfully used an old law to bring charges against him for attending auctions under an alias, Hylton switched from investigations to working mostly on outreach efforts at HSUS. He campaigned against cruelty happening in rodeos, and worked to make shelters and animal-control agencies nationwide more humane. He was later put in charge of building and running the agency's education center in Virginia. Hylton ended his long HSUS career as an accreditation officer, giving the official agency stamp of approval to shelters across the nation.

FROM BUTCHER BLOCK TO SOAP BOX

Tom Regan (1938–2017) was a moral philosopher who tackled a number of social justice issues, especially animal rights. He is best known for authoring *The Case for Animal Rights*. Regan had put himself through college by working as a butcher. "The pieces of meat I was working with might as well have been blocks of wood," he once told Sam Smith in an interview. After graduation, he began protesting the Vietnam War. Once he had made a connection between the violence of war and killing animals for meat, he started living as a strict vegetarian. The senseless loss of his dog after the animal was hit by a car drove home for Regan the fact that all animals had valuable lives, not just family pets.

In 1983, he published *The Case for Animal Rights*. The philosophical argument put forth in the book was that animals have value because they are sentient beings, and as such, their lives matter, particularly to the animals themselves. This is a state that Regan called being a "subject-of-a-life." The book caused a commotion in the animal welfare community, which considered reducing animals' suffering was more important than recognizing these creatures' rights.

ANIMAL ETHICS

Australian philosopher Peter Singer (1946–) is considered by many to be the father of the modern animal rights movement. His book, *Animal Liberation: A New Ethics for Our Treatment of Animals*, is a landmark work in the field. After befriending a group of vegetarian school chums, Singer began to question some of his life choices. He committed to a meat-free lifestyle while at

Oxford University in the late 1960s. Shortly after making that decision, he wrote *Animal Liberation*, which was first published in 1975. The book

Animal advocates may not always agree on the finer points of what rights nonhuman animals should have. They all agree that animals should at least be treated humanely.

reflected his belief in utilitarianism, which basically revolves around the principle that actions promoting happiness are right, and those that cause suffering are wrong. When animals suffer at the hands of humans, people are guilty of committing a grave wrong. Instead, animals should be treated humanely.

Singer did not advocate for animals having the same rights as humans. Rather, he argued that while they were not exactly the same, both human and nonhuman animals had the capacity for suffering—and because of that, equal consideration should be given to both with regard to ending or avoiding that condition. He was against speciesism, which involves showing preferential treatment based on a being's species. Most people considered humans to be superior to nonhuman animals based primarily, if not solely, on the fact that they are human. Speciesism, therefore, would grant rights to humans, but not to lesser beings such as animals.

Singer's utilitarian views on animal rights went largely unchallenged until the 1980s, when philosophers, such as Tom Regan, championed the view that animals had rights because they were "subject-of-a-life."

A ONE-MAN MOVEMENT

Longtime activist and campaign organizer Henry Spira (1927–1998) sometimes angered and alienated fellow animal rights activists. However, even those he upset could not argue with his skills and the many successes he scored over decades of social justice work.

Born in Belgium, Spira and his family moved to the United States prior to the start of World War II (1939–1945). He started his advocacy in animal rights later in life, at age forty-five. Before he fought against animal experimentation and cruelty inflicted upon farm animals, Spira had been engaged in other forms of social justice, namely the civil rights movement and labor issues. He joined the animal rights movement in the early 1970s, working (mostly alone) out of his New York City apartment under the organizational name of Animal Rights International.

His first campaign against animal cruelty was aimed at his adopted hometown's American Museum of Natural History. He worked to convince research scientists there to stop experimenting on live cats. And he succeeded. It was the first time in a long time that an animal advocacy campaign had effectively stopped an instance of animal experimentation. Spira also was the driving force behind efforts to get cosmetics companies to stop experiments on rabbits. He even persuaded many of those companies to help fund the creation of the Center for Alternatives to Animal Testing at Johns Hopkins University.

In the late 1970s, Spira successfully campaigned to require that hospitals and labs establish review boards to oversee their research practices. The boards were charged with making sure these institutions used animal-free, alternate methods of research whenever possible, and reducing the pain and suffering of animals that were used for research purposes. The latter portion of his campaigns sought to improve conditions for farm animals, ending the practice of branding cows on their faces and convincing fast-food restaurants to keep an eye out for how their suppliers treated livestock.

Spira's methods came under fire from groups such as People for the Ethical Treatment of Animals (PETA), which thought he should not negotiate or otherwise work with the people and organizations he was trying to reform. In turn, Spira openly criticized groups such as the Animal Liberation Front for the destructive and sometimes violent ways in which they advocated for animals. He much preferred publicity and negotiation to accomplish his goals—tactics that, in the end, worked very well for him.

WOMEN'S WORK

Caroline Earle White (1833–1916) was the driving force behind the creation of Pennsylvania's first animal welfare organization, and the nation's first animal shelter. Unfortunately, she was not able to enjoy proper acknowledgment of these accomplishments in her lifetime—because she was a woman.

White came from a family of Quakers who supported abolition, or the abolishment of slavery. Other family members were active in the movement to give women the right to vote. The plight of animals came to White's attention after seeing wagon drivers beat horses for supposedly not working hard enough. Using advice she got from Henry Bergh, who founded the American Society for the Prevention of Cruelty to Animals, she chartered the Pennsylvania version of the

Caroline White (*left front*, *seated*), posing with members of the International Anti-Vivisection Congress, worked behind the scenes, but was a powerful force in the early animal rights movement.

ASPCA. Fittingly, the PSPCA tackled working conditions for the city's horses as its top priority.

White's husband, Richard, took a seat on the board. But because she was a woman, White herself remained in the background, working to build the organization and recruit new members. To help

Caroline White fought for the establishment of shelters in Philadelphia, like today's Morris Animal Refuge—which sheltered this 2017 Puppy Bowl contestant, held by Philadelphia Eagle Mychal Kendricks.

give like-minded women more of a chance to participate in animal welfare issues, White started a women's branch of the organization, focused first and foremost on rescuing abused and stray dogs. The women raised funds for the first animal shelter built in the United States, which is still in operation outside Philadelphia.

Once the shelter was up and running, White had a conversation with a doctor who offered to take unwanted dogs off her hands, to be used for experimentation. Not only did she outright refuse the doctor, but the encounter led her to start an organization known as the American Anti-Vivisection Society in 1883. The group fought against the use of animals in medical experiments, bringing national attention to their cause when members handed out leaflets condemning vivisection at the 1893 Chicago World's Fair.

CHAPTER FOUR

ORGANIZATIONS AND THEIR ORGANIZERS

C oncern for animals has given rise to several organizations in the United States dedicated to overseeing animal welfare and fighting for their rights. Among them are a number of recognizable names—leaders in the field who are well respected, or at least well known, for how they have chosen to defend animals.

On the one hand, the American Society for the Prevention of Cruelty to Animals and the Humane Society of the United States are more traditional regarding the ways in which they guard the lives of nonhuman animals. PETA, on the other hand, takes a hardline stance with regard to animal rights, often incorporating rather extreme measures to further their cause. Mercy for Animals fights for the right of farm animals to live their lives free of suffering, while Farm Sanctuary is primarily geared toward offering safe shelter to rescued livestock.

Nonhuman animals are not the only objects of interest when discussing animal advocacy organizations. Often the lives and actions of the people

An animal rescue worker in Massachusetts getting to know donkeys rescued from an illegal petting zoo. Animal rights advocates often put their beliefs into action like this.

who founded these groups are as fascinating as the work of the organizations themselves—maybe even more so.

FIRST TO COMBAT CRUELTY IN AMERICA

Patterned after the Royal Society for the Prevention of Cruelty to Animals in England (RSPCA), the American Society for the Prevention of Cruelty to Animals (ASPCA) was formed in 1866 in New York City. Soon after the group had received its charter, the state legislature passed the country's first anticruelty law. This gave ASPCA officers the ability to investigate cases of animal cruelty and bring charges against offenders.

At first, the group concentrated on helping the horses that worked pulling carts, wagons, and carriages through the streets of the city. A year after receiving its charter, the ASPCA began operating an ambulance that could transport injured carthorses to a safe location. (The ambulance itself was pulled by healthy horses.) Later, several cities that had started ASPCA chapters petitioned their local and state governments to build fountains that served as watering stations for horses at work. Some cities organized annual workhorse parades, where groomed and decorated animals were admired by the public, raising people's appreciation for them. The first such parade was held in Boston in 1903.

Livestock were also on the newly formed ASPCA's radar. So were pet dogs that, at the time, were in danger of being stolen and not returned until a ransom was paid. Animal fighting was another form of cruelty tackled by ASPCA officers.

The group expanded its efforts to include steps toward helping to keep animals healthy. Starting with a clinic that saw to the medical needs of workhorses, the ASPCA incorporated veterinary care for abused and abandoned animals. Breakthroughs in surgical procedures, including making the use of an anesthetic a common occurrence, went beyond traditional means of dealing with sick or injured animals.

Since its beginning, the ASPCA has introduced and supported several animal welfare and anti-cruelty laws. These include the federal Animal Welfare Act of 1966, which set rules regarding the humane treatment of lab, zoo, and performing animals; 2007's Animal Fighting Prohibition Enforcement Act, which imposes harsher penalties for being involved in animal battles as a business; and the Veterinary Medicine Mobility Act (2014), which made it easier for veterinarians to treat animals outside their

ASPCA workers rescuing a dog in North Carolina, in the aftermath of 2016's Hurricane Matthew. Rescues are just one aspect of what the group does for animals.

clinics in emergency situations.

ASPCA officers are still very much on the job today, at the ready to rescue abused and neglected pets and livestock. Sometimes working with law enforcement, they work to shut down puppy mills, break up underground animal fighting rings, and investigate cases of suspected animal cruelty. The group has added animal rescue during natural disasters to its growing repertoire of services offered.

The ASPCA has spearheaded programs aimed at helping creatures find homes and live good lives after they had been rescued from dangerous situations. In an effort to cut down on the number of stray and unwanted household pets, the organization initiated a spay and neuter program. The group also has been at the forefront of offering classes that address behavioral and obedience issues in the hopes of making pets more adoptable, as well as helping troubled animals stay with their owners in what are meant to be forever homes.

A NOT-SO-DIPLOMATIC "MEDDLER"

The founder and driving force behind the ASPCA was Henry Bergh (1813–1888). Born into a wealthy shipbuilding family, Bergh had landed a position as a diplomat during Abraham Lincoln's administration, and was posted at the court of Russian Czar Alexander II. There he witnessed several instances of workhorses being beaten and otherwise abused by their owners. As the story goes, he was so moved by the abuse that he physically stopped a Russian carriage driver from whipping a horse that had fallen and could not continue working. Upon returning to New York City, Bergh resigned from the diplomatic corps, abandoning a rather promising career, to make caring for animals his life's mission.

As an animal advocate, Bergh was more likely to show his impassioned side than rely on his diplomatic training. Similar to when he had interfered with the Russian horse-beater, Bergh did not hesitate to physically confront animal abusers on the spot, making himself a target for harm in the process. Those he did not challenge in person were likely to get a scolding letter from him, calling them out for mistreating the animals in their care. In ASPCA annual reports, Bergh included the names of people who had been charged with crimes against animals.

Bergh's methods brought him plenty of attention—not all of it favorable. Newspapers of the time nicknamed him "The Great Meddler," because he was constantly putting himself in the middle of situations that people thought, at the time, were none of his business. Yet there were also a number of people who approved of Bergh, and many who supported the work of the ASPCA.

FIGHTING FOR HUMANE TREATMENT

Encouraged by the successes of the national ASPCA, a number of state animal welfare organizations joined forces in 1877 to form the American Humane Association (AHA). By the 1950s, it seemed as if the emphasis of both the ASPCA and the AHA was strongly on the sheltering and welfare of household pets. Several AHA members believed that the group must reinforce its commitment to other concerns, particularly standing up against animal experimentation. They split from the AHA and formed a new organization, the Humane Society of the United States (HSUS). The group was based in Washington, DC, but made excellent use of its state and local

NOT TESTED ON ANIMALS

NO ANIMAL INGREDIENTS

™

Made
Seven
60 Lake
Burling
©2010
Seven

Product proudly announcing its animal-cruelty-free origins. Groups such as HSUS are responsible for making the lack of animal testing a celebrated cause.

affiliates, which have grown considerably as the years have passed.

HSUS has been an animal welfare, not animal rights, agency from the beginning. Considerable time and resources went into the group's first large campaign to pass federal legislation aimed at decreasing animal suffering during slaughter. HSUS also fought against medical research companies that wanted to use shelter animals as the subjects of laboratory experiments. The organization would later campaign to end animal testing by cosmetics companies. Over the years, HSUS successes have included:

- convincing several food companies, supermarkets, and restaurant chains to purchase and use only cage-free eggs;
- helping governments ban seal products, crippling the seal-hunt industry;
- requiring that companies reduce or eliminate testing on animals, particularly chimpanzees;
- helping to change sentencing guidelines regarding animal fighting operations; and
- preserving wildlife habitats.

The organization is also known for conducting undercover investigations into cases of cruelty and neglect. With affiliates throughout the United States and a presence in eight additional countries, today's HSUS is one of the largest animal advocacy organizations in the world. As such, it is able to gain widespread support for its cause. The group drafts and supports proanimal legislation.

MAN OF ACTION

Before becoming the cofounder and the first executive director of the HSUS, Fred Myers (1904–1963) had worked as editor of the AHA's magazine. An experienced reporter who had covered many top stories of the day, Myers joined the group in 1952 to lend his journalism skills to a cause he cared about deeply. Within two years, however, he and AHA management had a falling out over the practice of pound seizure, where shelters were more or less forced to surrender animals under their care to laboratories conducting experiments. Disgusted that the organization was not taking a stronger stand against this practice, Myers led a group of like-minded AHA members—including future International Society for Animal Rights founder Helen Jones—to start a new animal advocacy organization. This group later became the modern-day HSUS.

Myers was known for not backing down from a fight. Accounts of his life have him taking active part in HSUS investigations, even helping to infiltrate and shut down a dog-fighting ring reportedly run by the Ku Klux Klan in Mississippi. Because of his passion for animals, Myers made

ANIMAL LEGAL DEFENSE FUND

In 1979, the Animal Legal Defense Fund (ALDF) was established to help enact and enforce laws to protect animals. The group prosecutes those accused of animal cruelty, sues people and organizations on behalf of animals, and encourages state and federal governments to strengthen penalties for harming pets, livestock, and wildlife. ALDF encourages law schools to include animal law courses in their curriculum. It also urges lawyers with the organization to help practicing attorneys with little experience in this area try animal cruelty cases—for free. Workshops, newsletters, training, and education programs make up the organization's outreach efforts.

a lot of enemies. People whom he had rubbed the wrong way labeled him a communist, which, during the 1950s, could ruin a person's career and life. No definite proof ever surfaced that linked Myers to the Communist Party, but the accusation alone caused damage to his reputation and that of the HSUS.

The stress from his work seems to have taken a toll on Myers. He had a heart attack in 1954, the year that HSUS was first formed, and another four years later. His third cardiac arrest was his last; he died in December 1963.

IN-YOUR-FACE ACTIVISM

In 1978, a young college student's visit to a slaughterhouse directly led to the creation of one of largest—and most recognizable—animal rights organizations in the world. The student in question was Alex Pacheco (1958–), and the organization he cofounded with British animal rights activist Ingrid Newkirk (1949–), was People for the Ethical Treatment of Animals, more commonly known as PETA.

The group came to the public's attention in a big way in 1981. PETA's main focus at the time was animal liberation, meaning animals were to be freed from being experimented on or used for food. The organization's first step toward making liberation a reality occurred at Maryland's Institute for Behavioral Research (IBR), where cofounder Pacheco had taken a job in order to better understand the type of battle PETA was fighting. Seventeen monkeys being held in tiny cages were subjected to gruesome experiments at an IBR lab. Pacheco took notes and pictures that showed horrible conditions at the lab and turned them over to the police. Law enforcement soon after raided the lab and brought charges against the lead researcher.

PETA publicity stunts, such as this 2016 skeletal crew of protesters in Hollywood, California, have gained attention—both good and bad—for the animal rights group.

Since then, PETA has waged campaigns against animals being used for experimentation, food, and entertainment purposes. They have won high-profile cases against additional federal research labs, including the National Aeronautics Space Administration (NASA), General Motors, major fast food and retail sales chains, and the United States Army. Despite these victories, the group is perhaps better known for using extreme stunts to publicize its cause. A longstanding PETA campaign against the use of fur in fashion featured ads with models posing nude. The models proclaimed they would rather go naked than wear fur. Less "sexy" tactics have involved throwing blood or "flour bombs" at people who are in favor of fur.

CONFRONTATIONAL AND CONTROVERSIAL

In 2000, Pacheco resigned from PETA due to concerns over the direction the organization was taking. When he started the group, he had planned to bring about change through investigations that exposed wrongdoing (like the one that started it all in Maryland), legal action, passing and enforcing proanimal laws, and educating the general public about animal rights. His cofounder, Newkirk, preferred the daring, sometimes way-over-the-top stunts she typically originated. These tactics have grown increasingly fanatical over the years, bringing PETA nearly as much negative publicity as they have support for the cause.

Controversy has plagued PETA in other areas as well. The organization as a whole, and Newkirk specifically, have been linked to the radical animal advocacy group Animal Liberation Front (ALF). The Federal Bureau of Investigations and the Department of Homeland Security in the United States regards ALF as a domestic terrorist group. Methods used by activists in the name of ALF, including destroying property and making death threats, earned the group that classification. ALF is not an organized group. Rather, membership is earned by taking action against people and organizations who they believe have made "slaves" of animals.

FOR LOVE OF HILDA

In 1986, volunteers with the newly formed animal advocacy group Farm Sanctuary began an investigation of a Pennsylvania stockyard—a place where farm animals were kept prior to being sold, transported elsewhere, or slaughtered. Among a pile of sheep bodies, they found a lamb that had been left for dead, struggling to raise her head. The organization's cofounder, Gene Baur, put her in his van and raced to the nearest veterinarian. The lamb, which was named Hilda, made a full recovery. She was placed on a farm in Watkins Glen, New York, making her the very first animal rescued by the group.

Farm Sanctuary was set up to do for animals being bred mainly for food what the ASCPA was doing for working animals and household pets, namely rescue and protect them. Their goal was evident in their name; they wanted to provide sanctuary for farm animals. Safety came in the form of farms that had been turned into shelters. Animals were made available for adoption, but if homes could not be found for them elsewhere, they were considered lifelong residents of a sanctuary farm. As of 2018, Farm Sanctuary operates three such shelters, two in California and the original in Watkins Glen.

Even before Hilda was found, Farm Sanctuary organizers felt there was a need to save livestock from cruel farming practices, such as dumping sick or injured animals like Hilda into dead piles. Members also have fought what is called agribusiness or factory farming, which involves treating animals more like end products

HAVE MERCY!

Nathan Runkle (1984–) grew up on a working farm in Ohio, so he had firsthand knowledge of how animals used for food were treated and slaughtered. But when he witnessed a fellow high school student's brutal attempt at killing a newborn piglet, which had been brought in by a teacher for agriculture students to dissect, he knew he had to take action. Runkle formed Mercy for Animals as a local, grassroots organization to raise awareness of cruel and inhumane farming practices. The movement grew, and today the organization is recognized for its work toward ending cruelty on the nation's farms and for helping people make "compassionate food choices."

As executive director, Runkle both ran Mercy for Animals and participated directly in its many campaigns, protests, and investigations. He was inducted into the United States Animal Rights Hall of Fame in 2009. In 2018, Runkle announced that he was stepping down as executive director of the nonprofit organization, but would remain active on the board. The move has allowed him to create other

(continued on the next page)

(continued from the previous page)

proanimal ventures, such as the Good Food Institute, which promotes healthy meat alternatives. Runkle also established the vegan food and music festival Circle V, the proceeds from which benefits Mercy for Animals.

than living beings. Farm Sanctuary has waged campaigns against such factory farming practices as force feeding animals or injecting them with drugs to make them fatter and produce more meat. It also works to get rid of small, crowded crates and cages that do not allow animals to walk around or sometimes even lay down. Members work with state governments to pass laws against these and similar practices.

Farm Sanctuary runs publicity campaigns and educational programs that aim to expose cruel farming practices, or describe what scientists have discovered about how animals think and feel. The group also introduces people to the benefits of a plant-based diet in a bid to get them to either stop eating meat or at least reduce the amount of animal product they consume. Like most animal welfare and rights groups, Farm Sanctuary is a nonprofit organization that relies on donations from the public to continue operating. Fittingly, the group's biggest

Mercy for Animals founder Nathan Runkle addressing the media at a press conference discussing undercover investigations by animal rights advocate groups, in Los Angeles, California, 2015.

donors belong to Hilda's Club, named after the tiny lamb that started it all.

HOT DOG!

Gene Baur (1962–) is an advocate willing to put his money where his mouth is—and he's hoping that the mouths of others will follow suit. A vegan since 1985, Baur was able to start the animal welfare group Farm Sanctuary with funding gained from selling meatless "hot dogs" at Grateful Dead concerts beginning in the late 1980s. If he was able to convince some of the customers and others he met along the way to adopt a vegan lifestyle as well, then all the better.

A native of Hollywood, California, Baur put himself through school working as a background actor appearing in, among other things, fast food commercials. An interest in agribusiness led him to add a master's degree from Cornell University to his bachelor's degree in sociology. He began working for environmental and human rights causes as a young man but developed a laser focus on bettering the lives of farm animals about the same time he became vegan and started Farm Sanctuary.

Baur's hands-on approach to animal advocacy was first apparent when he physically loaded the downed lamb Hilda into his Volkswagen van, and rushed her to the doctor. That same dedication has been evident as Baur has continued to act on behalf of livestock. He photographs and videotapes cruel farming practices, testifying at trials and during legislative votes and helping to introduce a veggie burger onto the Burger King menu. In 2011, to celebrate Farm Sanctuary's twenty-fifth anniversary, Baur climbed back into his VW van and traveled cross-country on what he called the Just Eats Tour. He spoke with people who had embraced veganism and posted regularly to the Farm Sanctuary website so that everyone sympathetic to the group's cause could share in the journey.

CHAPTER FIVE

HOW TO GET INVOLVED

C aring about animals is arguably the first and most important step one can take toward getting involved in the animal rights movement. Everything else kind of stems from this, including stating the case for animals that cannot speak for themselves and taking action to support one's beliefs. Those two means of involvement, speaking out and stepping up, are referred to as advocacy and activism, respectively.

Figuring out how involved one wants to get in the animal rights movement ultimately determines the exact steps a person will take. Becoming part of the movement can be accomplished as part of a group or as a single individual. It can involve personal beliefs and public acts. A willingness to read, listen, and learn will take a person far as he or she joins a social justice cause such as animal rights. Most of all, though, anyone looking to become an advocate or activist for animals should be willing to devote time and energy to the cause.

Protesters demonstrating against the sale of fur. In general, the more people who gather to speak their minds, the more legitimate the cause may seem to outsiders.

COME TOGETHER

One person's opinion is mainly that—a single opinion. But a bunch of people with the same opinion, who are willing to act on their beliefs, is a movement. Getting involved frequently means working with other like-minded people. The benefit to such a situation is that more can get done more easily, and in a shorter amount of time. As the old saying goes, many hands make light work.

Another advantage of being in an animal rights organization is that people are more likely to take a group and their message seriously. Groups are harder to dismiss than individuals. Think about how politicians might view one or two people in the waiting room of their office, wanting to discuss animal rights, versus being faced with a group of protestors marching in the streets outside that same office.

Finding people who think the same way about animals in your area should not be difficult. If you feel as if you cannot find just the right group, however, or members seem to be too scattered or distant to make meeting regularly a possibility, you can always try starting your own animal rights group. This can be done informally at first, with group members getting together and helping animals in small ways. The longer a group stays together and the larger its membership gets, the greater the chance that you might want to consider writing up a charter and making it an official animal rights organization.

Before joining or supporting any kind of social justice movement, it is important to know as much as possible about them and how they operate. Do some homework by reading up on their history or scrolling around their website. Check to see if they are legitimate and if their methods and style are to your liking. For instance, PETA has affected change with regards to animal rights over the years, but their approach is very confrontational and flashy. They may not be the best fit for someone who is laid-back, or prefers behind-the-scenes advocacy. Likewise, you are better off steering clear of groups that use violence or illegal activity to get their point across to the masses. Choose well, choose wisely.

SPEAK OUT, SPEAK UP

One tried and true form of activism is protesting. This involves expressing your opinion for or against an action or policy in public, with the objective of raising awareness and support. Protestors may carry signs with images and slogans, pass out literature about their cause, chant, or make speeches. Organizing a protest takes time and planning, so that things do not turn ugly and get out of hand. To avoid fights or possibly arrests, protests should be organized and peaceful. A few good rules of thumb are to make sure your group has a legal right to be

High school students in Virginia practicing their photography skills as a way to help model Rosie and her shelter friends get adopted.

on the property where the protest is being held, not block car or foot traffic, and not engage in shouting or punching matches with people who do not agree with you.

You also can let your voice be heard without actually speaking. Write a letter to the editor stating your point of view. You might also write to your local, state, or federal governmental representatives, as a

ONE DAY MEAT FREE

Not ready to become a vegetarian or vegan right away? Try dipping your toe in the flesh-free lifestyle by simply reducing your consumption of animal products. One way to do this is to voluntarily take part in the international Meatless Monday movement. Meatless Monday traces its

For more than a decade, people have been participating in New York City's Veggie Pride Parade, which seeks to raise awareness of a meat-free lifestyle.

roots to an American effort during World War I (1914–1918) to ration food so that the United States would have enough to feed its troops overseas as well as its allies in Europe. The current campaign originally was not designed to convert people to vegetarianism, but to help them make healthier food choices. Concerns for animal welfare also played a part in the campaign.

way to influence laws that are favorable to the movement. Social media posts are also an option.

Of course, you also should speak up when you see an injured animal, or witness abuse or neglect. Humane societies, shelters, animal control offices, and even the police can either directly help in this regard or point you in the right direction to make a report of suspected cruelty.

ESCHEW YOUR FOOD

Many committed animal rights activists have been known to eschew, or deliberately avoid, eating meat on principle. They follow either a vegetarian or vegan diet, which is plant based. Vegetarians do not eat meat, and they also may not consume any animal products, including animal milk (lacto-vegetarian) and eggs (ovo-vegetarian). Being vegan goes beyond diet and is more accurately described as a lifestyle. In addition to not eating anything that either was or comes from an animal, vegans also do not use animal products in clothing, cosmetics, etc. Keep in mind that food products are not the only source of concern for vegans and vegetarians. Even medications may use animal products, such as the gelatin that either coats pills or makes up a capsule.

The animal-free lifestyle takes a bit of work, at least at first. Animal products are sometimes hidden in long lists of ingredients, so reading labels becomes important. Do a little research and ask questions, too. Among the online resources that can help those new to the vegetarian or vegan lifestyle is the website of The Vegetarian Resource Group (www.vrg.org). The organization posts a list of ingredients to avoid, as well as vegetarian and vegan recipes and more.

COMMIT TO COMMITTING

No matter how deeply you choose to get involved in the animal rights movement, it is important that

Animals often must depend on the kindness of volunteers and advocates for food, safe shelter, and the chance to live a happy, pain-free life.

you make your involvement your own. Your contributions to the cause can be as individual as you are. In addition to the suggestions already mentioned, you could organize a bake sale to raise money for an animal welfare/rights group. Or, raise funds so that your class can sponsor a shelter or farm animal on a monthly basis. Get friends to sign a petition pledging to go meatless at least once a week. Volunteer to use your excellent design skills to brighten up the website of an animal-focused nonprofit. There are all sorts of ways to get involved and make a difference. Be creative. But above all, if you really believe in the animal rights movement, make the commitment to stand by your principles and take action.

TIMELINE

1866 The American Society for the Prevention of Cruelty to Animals (ASPCA) receives its charter. Originally focused on horses, the group later expands its reach to most other animals.

1871 Charles Darwin's *The Descent of Man*, which highlighted similarities among "higher primates," meaning the great apes and humans, is published.

1954 The Humane Society of the United States (HSUS) founded. Seeking to work on a national level, the group bases its operations in Washington, DC.

1964 Ruth Harrison's *Animal Machines* exposes animal cruelty in farming.

1966 The Animal Welfare Act is passed in the United States. It is the first, and only, federal animal protection law in the nation.

1975 Peter Singer publishes *Animal Liberation*, an important and inspirational book in the animal rights movement.

1978 Alex Pacheco cofounds People for the Ethical Treatment of Animals (PETA) with Ingrid Newkirk.

1979 Animal Legal Defense Fund (ALDF) is formed, helping to shape the state of animal law in the United States.

The Farm Animal Welfare Council in England releases a report that eventually forms the framework for the animal rights guidelines known as the Five Freedoms.

1986 Farm Sanctuary is formed; rescues its first animal, Hilda the sheep.

1999 Teenager Nathan Runkle starts the grassroots group Mercy for Animals, with the goal of helping farm animals.

2007 Animal Fighting Prohibition Enforcement Act is passed.

2009 The European Union approves the Lisbon Treaty, which included an article acknowledging animal sentience.

2013 The Nonhuman Rights Project files the first of several writs of habeas corpus, for a chimpanzee named Tommy. It is believed to be the first time such a legal tactic has been used on behalf of an animal.

2014 Veterinary Medicine Mobility Act is passed.

GLOSSARY

abandonment The withdrawal of protection, support, or care.

accreditation Official approval or authorization.

adaptations Biological adjustments to one's surroundings or environment.

advocate One who pleads the case of another.

ancestry One's line of descent; personal history of where someone came from.

anesthetic A solution to numb the body and/or reduce consciousness.

charter Written authorization to create a new organization.

cognitive Having to do with conscious thought and reasoning.

counterpart Someone or something that is incredibly similar to another person or thing.

ethical That which determines if an action is morally right or wrong.

evolution The scientific theory explaining how species began and moved to their present state.

fanatical Exhibiting extreme enthusiasm.

habitat The environment in which plants and animals live and grow.

infiltrate To secretly enter into a group or situation in order to weaken or otherwise change it.

neglect The state of being left alone without attention or care.

neurons Cells that send and receive nerve signals, allowing the nervous system to function.

primates Mammals that are highly developed and intelligent.

sanctuary A place that offers safety and comfort.

slaughter The killing of animals for food.

speciesism A prejudice in favor of one species over all others; theory of human superiority.

sentience The ability to feel and to be aware of oneself and the surroundings.

writ An official document sent and sealed by a government or court.

American Anti-Vivisection Society (AAVS)
801 Old York Road, Suite 204
Jenkintown, PA 19046-1611
(800) SAY-AAVS (729-2287)
Website: http://aavs.org
Facebook: @AmericanAntiVivisectionSociety
Twitter: @AAVS_AAVS
Founded in 1883, the AAVS seeks to end the use
of animals in medical testing and research.
In particular, the group's campaigns target
unlicensed animal dealers, the use of pound
seizures, and animal alteration, such as clon-
ing and genetic engineering. AAVS also has
worked to modify the Animal Welfare Act to
cover a broader range of lab animals.

Animal Alliance of Canada (AAC)
#101-221 Broadview Avenue
Toronto, ON M4M 2G3
Canada
(416) 462-9541
Website: https://www.animalalliance.ca
Facebook: @AnimalAllianceofCanada
Twitter: @Animal_Alliance
Instagram: @animalalliance
YouTube: AACoffice
Email: contact@animalalliance.ca
Founded in 1990, the AAC is a nonprofit organiza-
tion that seeks to protect all animals, as well as

promotes healthy working relationships among humans, nonhumans, and the environment. In addition helping to keep animals out of research labs, members lobby for legislation that takes the lives and welfare of animals into consideration.

Animal Welfare Foundation of Canada (AWFC)
Suite #643 – 280 Nelson Street
Vancouver, BC V6B 2E2
Canada
Website: http://awfc.ca
Facebook: @animalwelfarecanada
Email: awfc.info@gmail.com
The Animal Welfare Foundation of Canada attempts to get the Canadian public to consider the lives of animals before using them to human benefit. The group offers educational programs, research opportunities, and public outreach initiatives.

Canadian Federation of Humane Societies (CFHS)
30 Concourse Gate, 102
Ottawa, ON K2E 7V7
Canada
(613) 224-8072
Website: https://www.cfhs.ca
Facebook: @HumaneCanada
Twitter: @CFHS

Instagram: @humancanada
Email: info@cfhs.ca
The Canadian Federation of Humane Societies
    acts as an oversight group for animal welfare
    groups across Canada. Caring for companion
    and farm animals, the group focuses on policy,
    research, and matters of animal law.

The Dolphin Project
171 Pier Avenue, Box 234
Santa Monica, CA 90405
Website: https://www.dolphinproject.com
Facebook: @RicOBarrysDolphinProject
Twitter: @Dophin_Project
Instagram: @thedolphinproject
Email: contact@dolphinproject.com
Former dolphin trainer Ric O'Barry founded the
    Dolphin Project in 1970. The group's mission is
    to rehabilitate captive dolphins, stop the sense-
    less slaughter of commercial dolphin hunts,
    and educate the public about these incredibly
    intelligent creatures.

Farm Animal Rights Movement (FARM)
10101 Ashburton Lane
Bethesda, MD 20817
(888) FARM USA (327-6872)
Website: http://www.farmusa.org
Facebook: @farmanimalrights

Twitter and Instagram: @farmusa
Email: info@farmusa.org
FARM promotes a vegan lifestyle and raises public awareness of the cruelty found throughout
a farming industry that values profits over
animals' lives and well-being. Through class-
room presentations and handing out vegan
food samples, FARM reaches out to teens and
young adults, hoping to instill compassion for
nonhumans in the next generation.

Performing Animal Welfare Society (PAWS)
PO Box 849
Galt, CA 95632
(209) 745-2606
Website: http://www.pawsweb.org
Facebook: @pawsweb.org
Twitter: @PAWSARK2000
Instagram: @performinganimalwelfaresociety
Email: info@pawsweb.org
PAWS offers sanctuary to animals that have been
part of performing organizations, such as
circuses, as well as abused and neglected
wildlife. Founded in 1984, the group also offers
education and public awareness programs to
members of the entertainment industry, legisla-
tors, and the general public.

FOR FURTHER READING

Armstrong, Susan J., and Richard G. Botzler, eds. *Animal Ethics Reader.* Florence, KY: Routledge, 2016.

Berlatsky, Noah. *Animal Rights* (Current Controversies). Farmington Hills, MI: Greenhaven Press, 2015.

Keim, Brandon, et. al. *National Geographic Inside Animal Minds: What They Think, Feel, and Know.* Des Moines, IA: National Geographic Books, 2017.

Kluger, Jeffrey. *The Animal Mind: How They Think. How They Feel. How to Understand Them.* New York, NY: Time Home Entertainment, Inc., 2017.

Pacelle, Wayne. *The Humane Economy: How Innovators and Enlightened Consumers Are Transforming the Lives of Animals.* New York, NY: HarperCollins Publishers, 2016.

Regan, Tom. *Empty Cages: Facing the Challenge of Animal Rights.* Lanham, MD: Rowman & Littlefield Publishers, Inc., 2004.

Silvey, Anita. *Untamed: The Wild Life of Jane Goodall.* Washington, DC: National Geographic Society, 2015.

Singer, Peter. Alex Pacheco*: The Definitive Classic of the Animal Movement.* New York, NY: HarperCollins Publishers, 2009.

Waldau, Paul. *Animal Rights: What Everyone Needs to Know.* New York, NY: Oxford University Press, 2011.

BIBLIOGRAPHY

Beers, Diane L. *For the Prevention of Cruelty: The History and Legacy of Animal Rights Activism in the United States*. Athens, OH: Swallow Press/Ohio University Press, 2006.

Bekoff, Marc. "After 2,500 Studies, It's Time to Declare Animal Sentience Proven." LiveScience, September 6, 2013. http://chq .org/40-season/schools/school-of-art/89-the-art -program.

Bekoff, Marc, and Jessica Pierce. *The Animals' Agenda: Freedom, Compassion, and Coexistence in the Human Age*. Boston, MA: Beacon Press, 2017.

Bernstein, Adam. "R. Dale Hylton, 77; Animal Rights Advocate." *Washington Post,* February 9, 2008. https://patch.com/us/across-america /tom-regan-moral-philosopher-animal-rights -pioneer-dies-78.

Conklin, Tina. "An animal welfare history lesson on the Five Freedoms." Michigan State University Extension, February 25, 2014. http://msue.anr .msu.edu/news/an_animal_welfare_history _lesson_on_the_five_freedoms.

Feder, Barnaby J. "Henry Spira, 71, Animal Rights Crusader." *New York Times,* September 15, 1998. http://www.nytimes.com/1998/09/15 /business/henry-spira-71-animal-rights -crusader.html.

Fenwick, Cody. "Tom Regan, Moral Philosopher

and Animal Rights Pioneer, Dies at 78." Across America Patch, February 18, 2017. https://patch .com/us/across-america/tom-regan -moral-philosopher-animal-rights -pioneer-dies-78.

Gould, James L., and Carol Grant. "Reasoning In Animals." *Scientific American*, Vol. 9, No. 4, 1998, pp. 52–59.

Haines, Lester. "Cows bear grudges: official." The Register, March 2005. https://www.theregister .co.uk/2005/03/04/cows_bear_grudges.

Hoole, Jan. "Here's What the Science Says About Sentience." The Conversation, November 24, 2017. https://theconversation.com /heres-what-the-science-says-about-animal -sentience-88047.

Kelly, Kate. "First Animal Shelter in U.S. Due to Caroline Earle White." America Comes Alive, March 18, 2016. https://americacomesalive .com/2016/03/18/first-animal-shelter-u-s-due -caroline-earle-white.

Kelly, Kate. "Harriet Lawrence Hemenway (1858-1960): saving Birds One Hat at a Time." American Comes Alive, April 8, 2014. https:// americacomesalive.com.

Kerns, Ben. "9 Animals Who Have More In Common With Humans Than You Think." The Dodo, May 29, 2015. https://www.thedodo.com /animals-you-had-no-idea-were-so-closely

-related-to-humans-1172946617.html.

Kiter, Tammy. "Henry Bergh: Angel in Top Hat of the Great Meddler?" New York Historical Society, March 21, 2012. http://blog.nyhistory .org/henry-bergh-angel-in-top-hat-or-the -great-meddler.

Nadon, M. Michelle. "It's Time to Modernize Animal Rights In Canada With Bill C-246." Huffington Post, July 4, 2016. http://www .huffingtonpost.ca/m-michelle-nadon /animal-rights-canada_b_10774816.html.

Querna, Betsy. "Dolphins Recognize, Admire Themselves in Mirrors, Study Finds." National Geographic News, May 2, 2001. https://news .nationalgeographic.com/news/2001/05/0502 _dolphinvanity.html.

Robertson, Lori. "Are rodeos a form of culture or cruelty?" BBC, February 8, 2012. http://www .bbc.com/travel/story/20120207-ethical -traveller-are-rodeos-a-form-of-culture-or -cruelty.

Staff. "Farmed Animals and the Law." Animal League Defense Fund. Retrieved March 18, 2018. http://aldf.org/resources /advocating-for-animals/farmed-animals-and -the-law.

Staff. "How Genetically Related Are We to Bananas?" Get Science, June 29, 2017. https:// www.getscience.com/content/how

-genetically-related-are-we-bananas.

Staff. "How to Start an Animal Rights Group in 5 Steps." PETA, May 2, 2014. https://www.peta .org/action/activism-guide/start-animal-rights -group.

Staff. "Our Clients." Nonhuman Rights Project, Retrieved March 18, 2018. https://www .nonhumanrights.org/litigation.

Wolchover, Natalie. "When Will We Learn to Speak Animal Languages?" LiveScience, August 17, 2012. https://www.livescience.com/22474 -animal-languages-communication.html.

Yount, Lisa. *Animal Rights*. New York, NY: Facts on File, 2004.

INDEX

ABOUT THE AUTHOR

Jeanne Nagle is a writer, editor, and animal lover living in upstate New York. She is the author of several books on the animal kingdom, as well as social justice issues. Among the titles she has written are *How Do Animals Hunt and Feed?*, *Saving the Endangered American Alligator*, and *Coping with the Threat of Deportation*.

PHOTO CREDITS

Cover (top) B. Anthony Stewart/National Geographic/Getty Images; cover (bottom) Kevork Djansezian/Getty Images; p. 3 Rawpixel.com /Shutterstock.com; pp. 4-5 (background) Young Sam Green/EyeEm /Getty Images; p. 5 (inset) 9387388673/Shutterstock.com; pp. 8, 23, 43, 60, 84 NASA; p. 10 Abeselom Zerit/Shutterstock.com; p. 13 Stock Montage/Archive Photos/Getty Images; pp. 15, 41, 45, 58, 64-65, 88-89 © AP Images; p. 17 Rick Friedman/Corbis Historical /Getty Images; p. 20 Panos Karas/Shutterstock.com; p. 24 Corbis Historical/Getty Images; p. 27 leungchopan/Shutterstock.com; p. 29 Irma07/Shutterstock.com; p. 33 Bloomberg/Getty Images; p. 39 NurPhoto/Getty Images; p. 47 Culture Club/Hulton Archive/ Getty Images; pp. 52-53 Twinsterphoto/Shutterstock.com; p. 57 Library of Congress Prints and Photographs; p. 61 The Boston Globe/Getty Images; pp. 68-69 BirchTree/Alamy Stock Photo; pp. 74-75 Rodin Eckenroth/Getty Images; p. 81 Araya Diaz/Getty Images; p. 85 Richard Levine/Corbis News/Getty Images; p. 90 Pacific Press/LightRocket/Getty Images; pp. 92-93 a katz/Shutterstock .com.

Design: Michael Moy; Editor: Erin Staley; Photo Researcher: Nicole DiMella